Soups
&
Salads

TARLA DALAL

<u>S&C</u>

Fourth Printing : 1997

By the same author
The Pleasures of Vegetarian Cooking (Hindi, Gujarati, Russian)
The Delights of Vegetarian Cooking (Hindi, Gujarati)
The Joys of Vegetarian Cooking (Hindi)
Exciting Vegetarian Cooking (Hindi, Gujarati)
Low Calorie Healthy Cooking (Hindi, Gujarati, Marathi)
Microwave Cooking (Hindi)
Party Cooking (Hindi)
Eat Your Way to Good Health (Co-authored by Dr.Swati Piramal)
Quick & Easy Vegetarian Cookery
Desi Khana (Hindi, Gujarati, Marathi)
Chinese Cooking (Hindi)
Soups & Salads (Hindi)
Mocktails & Snacks
Rotis & Subzees (Hindi)
Tava Cooking
Mexican Cooking

Price Rs. 170/-

Published & Distributed by :
Sanjay & Company,
353, A-1, Shah & Nahar Industrial Estate, Dhanraj Mill Compound,
Lower Parel (W), Mumbai - 400 013.
Tel.: (91-22) 496 8068   Fax No.: (91-22) 496 5876 Email: sd@giasmbm 01.vsnl.net.in

Delhi Distributor :
Mr. Om Arora for Variety Book Depot
A.V.G.Bhavan, M-3 Con-Circle, P.O.Box 505, New Delhi 110 001.
Tel: (91-11) 332 7175/332 2567 Fax: (91-11) 371 4335

Western Region Distributor :
Wilco International
33, Rope Walk Lane, Off Rampart Row, ITTS House Fort, Mumbai 400 023
Tel: (91-22) 2041420/2042574 Fax: (91-22) 2041429 Email: wilco @bom2.vsnl.net.in

Printed by : **Magnum Prints**
G-4 Gandhi Nagar Shivner Marg, Lower Parel, Mumbai - 400 013 Tel: (91-22) 492 7672

Designed By : **Niranjan Kamatkar**

Photographs by : **Rajiv Asgaonkar**

Food Stylist : **Rohit Chawla**

ISBN No. 81-86469-02-8

CONTENTS

Salad Dressings

SOUPS

In this book, you will find a variety of vegetarian soups ranging from clear soups to creamy soups and thick vegetable chowders which are sufficiently filling and nutritious to be served as a meal by themselves. There are numerous nourishing every-day soups as well as rich party soups. All are tasty and most are simple to prepare. If you are an imaginative cook, you can use the recipes to turn out at least twice this number using your own ideas and variations. If however, you happen to be a novice cook, this book should help to make you an expert one. I am one of those who believes that a cup of hot (or for that matter chilled) soup, rightly flavoured, is welcome any day any time.

Two types of soup stocks are given in this book. Use them as mentioned in the recipes. The advent of stock cubes has made soup-making a great deal simpler for those in a hurry. However, you will find it more rewarding to make your own stock and keep a supply ready for use at any time. Home-made stock is not only simple to make as a perfect base for numerous soups but it can moreover be stored for long periods in the deep freeze.

A final word regarding serving. Hot soups are best served piping hot. Make sure they are never served lukewarm as otherwise, the soups may lose half their charm and taste. To bring out the best in soups, serve them with accompaniments such as chopped mint, grated cheese, cream, croutons, warm toast or garlic bread. It will make all the difference.

SALADS

Today's salads no longer merit the deprecating and patronising nomenclature of ``grass'' food. Indeed, salads have no limitations. They can be served at the start of a meal or even as a complete meal by themselves. No other combination of food or food products can compete as regards freedom to innovate and to choose from a wide variety of ingredients and flavours. Salads are moreover of great importance because of their food value with the result that people are increasingly realising the importance of eating salads.

This book contains a variety of tasty salads which are easy to make. Whichever the salad you make, remember the following:

1. Always select fresh and firm vegetables and fruits. Start with the best quality and handle the ingredients carefully and correctly so that there is no loss of nutrients.

2. When putting a salad together, think like an artist. Work towards a contrast of colours, flavours and shapes.

3. Whether using fresh, frozen or canned foods, ensure that the salad has eye appeal.

4. Garnish simply but attractively. Do not waste time in decorating lavishly. Leave that to the restaurants.

5. All the dressings in the book are without eggs. They include some low calorie dressings. Do take care to choose a dressing which matches the salad.

6. Drain the vegetables and fruits thoroughly before mixing with the dressing.

7. Except for hot salads, ensure that the salads are always served chilled.

How to store

1. Place the vegetables and fruits in the crisper and refrigerate, removing only unusable outer leaves. To prepare iceberg lettuce for crisping, remove only bruised leaves, separate the leaves properly and place in ice-cold water for at least 25 minutes.

2. Drain the vegetables and fruits thoroughly. Wrap loosely in a clean towel and place them in the refrigerator.

3. Vegetables like baby corn, french beans, etc. should be cooked for a few minutes on a high flame. Baby corn takes about two minutes to cook while french beans and cauliflower take a little longer. Ensure that you do not overcook any vegetables.

Herbs for salads

The variety of fresh herbs available in India is limited. The commonly available herbs are dill, coriander, mint and parsley. In place of basil, you can use fresh tulsi leaves.

Care of a wooden salad bowl

It is indeed a pleasure to use a good wooden salad bowl. Here are a few tips to keep it in good condition :

1. After each use, give a quick wash with warm soapy water, rinse quickly and dry thoroughly. Rub the inside with oil using soft paper.

2. Never put a wooden bowl into the refrigerator for chilling.

Salad secrets

1. If the mayonnaise is very thick, thin it by adding a little milk and mixing well.

2. If using fresh parsley in salad dressings, put it in hot water before chopping. This gives more flavour.

3. To cut parsley, dill etc., use scissors whenever possible.

4. To clean mushrooms, put them in a bowl of water, add one tablespoon of plain flour and rub with your hands.

5. To keep fruits from discolouring, peel and slice with a stainless steel knife in lemon juice.

6. To make croutons, cut the bread slices (try to use one-day old slices) and toast them in the oven.

SOUPS

✢ CORN CHOWDER ✢

PICTURE ON PAGE 18

A typical American-style thick soup with a pleasant hint of celery.

| Preparation time : 5 minutes. | Cooking time : 15 minutes. | Serves 6. |

1   teacup cooked corn
4   teacups white stock, page 26
1   onion, chopped
2   tablespoons chopped celery
2   tablespoons plain flour
2   teacups milk
1   tablespoon butter
    salt, pepper and nutmeg
    powder to taste

For the garnish

1   tablespoon chopped celery, lightly blanched
2   tablespoons tomato cubes (optional)
2   teaspoons grated cheese

1. Heat the butter in a pan, add the onion and celery and sauté till the onions are transparent.
2. Stir in the flour and remove from the heat. Add the stock and milk gradually.
3. Return to the heat and simmer gently for 5 minutes.
4. Add the corn, salt, pepper and nutmeg powder and simmer for another 10 minutes.

✢ **Serve hot, garnished with the blanched celery, tomato cubes and grated cheese.**

✤ CREAM OF BROCCOLI SOUP ✤

A healthy soup.

| Preparation time : 15 minutes. | Cooking time : 15 minutes. | Serves 6. |

1 teacup broccoli florets
3 tablespoons chopped onions
2 tablespoons plain flour
3 teacups milk
2½ teacups white stock, page 26
3 tablespoons butter
    salt, pepper and nutmeg
    powder to taste

1. Heat 1½ tablespoons of butter and sauté the onions lightly.
2. Add three fourths of the broccoli and cook gently for a few minutes. Add the stock and cook until soft. Remove from the heat and pass through a blender to make a purée.
3. Melt the remaining butter in a pan over gentle heat. Add the flour and stir for 1 minute making sure that there is no discolouration.
4. Add the milk and bring to the boil. Simmer for 5 minutes and add salt, pepper and nutmeg powder. Add to the soup.
5. In a separate pan of boiling water, blanch the remaining broccoli to a bright green colour. Strain carefully and refresh in ice-cold water. Drain.
6. Put the blanched broccoli in the soup, garnish and heat for a few minutes just before serving.

✤ **Serve piping hot.**

✥ WINTER VEGETABLE SOUP ✥

PICTURE ON BACK COVER

Swimming with cheese, this colourful soup makes a meal by itself.

Preparation time : 20 minutes.	Cooking time : 1 hour.	Serves 6.

3 tablespoons haricot beans (chawli)
$\frac{1}{2}$ teacup french beans, chopped
$\frac{1}{2}$ teacup carrot cubes
$\frac{1}{2}$ teacup potato cubes
$\frac{1}{2}$ teacup cauliflower florets
$\frac{1}{2}$ teacup tomato cubes, without seeds
1 teacup shredded cabbage
1 onion, chopped

$\frac{1}{4}$ teacup celery stalks
2 bay leaves
1 tablespoon butter
salt and pepper to taste

For the garnish

2 tablespoons chopped parsley
2 tablespoons grated cheese

1. Soak the haricot beans in water for 3 to 4 hours.
2. Heat the butter in a pan and fry the onion, celery and bay leaves lightly. Add the french beans, carrots, potatoes, harricot beans and cauliflower and cook for 5 to 7 minutes.
3. Add 6 cups of water and cook on a medium flame for 30 to 45 minutes until the beans are tender. Drain.
4. Add the cabbage and tomato cubes and cook for 3 to 4 minutes.
5. Add salt and pepper.

✥ **Serve hot, garnished with the chopped parsley and grated cheese.**

✤ CREAMY ALMOND SOUP ✤

PICTURE ON PAGE 37

Rich and tasty, having the delicate flavour of almonds.

Preparation time : 10 minutes.   **Cooking time : 20 minutes.**   **Serves 6.**

15	to 20 almonds	1	teacup milk
6	teacups white stock, page 26	3	to 4 drops almond essence
1	tablespoon plain flour	2	tablespoons butter
¼	teacup fresh cream		salt and pepper to taste

1. Soak the almonds in hot water for 10 minutes. Remove the skin. Keep aside a few and blend the rest to a fine purée in a liquidiser along with a little stock.

2. Add the almond paste to the white stock.

3. Melt the butter gently in a pan. Add the flour and stir till you get the cooked flour flavour, taking care that the flour does not discolour.

4. Add the stock and simmer for 10 minutes. Add the hot milk, almond essence, salt and pepper.

5. Cut the remaining almonds into slivers and bake them in an oven until crisp.

6. Add the cream on top of the soup.

✤ **Serve hot garnished with the almond slivers.**

BROWN ONION SOUP WITH PEPPER CHEESE BALLS

PICTURE ON PAGE 28

An exciting variation of the famous French onion soup.

Preparation time : 10 minutes.	Cooking time : 20 minutes.	Serves 6.

3 onions, sliced
2 teaspoons cornflour
3 tablespoons butter
   salt and pepper to taste

For the cheese balls

6 tablespoons grated cheese
2 crushed peppercorns
2 teaspoons chopped parsley

For the garnish

1 tablespoon chopped parsley

1. Heat the butter and fry the onions on a low flame for 10 to 15 minutes until golden brown in colour.
2. Add 5 cups of water, salt and pepper and bring to the boil.
3. Mix the cornflour in 1 cup of water and add to the soup. Simmer for 5 minutes.
4. Knead the ingredients for the cheese balls very well and shape into small balls.
5. Add the cheese balls to the soup just before serving.

❖ **Serve hot, garnished with the chopped parsley.**

✥ SPINACH AND BABY CORN SOUP ✥

PICTURE ON PAGE 27

Colourful, nutritious and crunchy.

Preparation time : 10 minutes.　　**Cooking time : 15 minutes.**　　**Serves 6.**

3 teacups white stock, page 26	1 tablespoon butter
15 to 20 big bright green spinach leaves, torn into 4	$\frac{1}{2}$ teaspoon freshly ground pepper
12 pieces baby corn	salt to taste
1 tablespoon cornflour	
1 chopped spring onion (with greens)	**For the garnish**
2 large garlic cloves	desiccated coconut (optional)
$\frac{1}{2}$ tablespoon Tabasco sauce	

1. Trim and wash the spinach, discarding any thick or tough stalks. Wash and cut the baby corn into bite-size chunks.
2. Dissolve the cornflour in a little stock.
3. Melt the butter in a pan. Add the onion and garlic and fry gently for 1 minute until soft, taking care that they do not discolour.
4. Add the baby corn and stir gently for 2 minutes.
5. Add the spinach and stir for a further 2 minutes.
6. Pour in the stock, 3 cups of water and the cornflour and bring to the boil while stirring throughout. Simmer for 5 minutes.
7. Add the Tabasco sauce, salt and pepper.

✥ **Serve hot, garnished with desiccated coconut.**

✣ HERBAL LENTIL SOUP ✣

An unusual combination of lentils, vegetables and fresh herbs makes this soup both colourful and tasty.

Preparation time : 10 minutes.   **Cooking time : 20 minutes.**   **Serves 6.**

1   onion, chopped
1   tablespoon chopped celery
2   tablespoons chopped dill
    or parsley
3   teaspoons cornflour
1   tablespoon butter
    salt and pepper to taste

For the stock

4   tablespoons moong dal
1   onion, chopped
1   potato, diced

For the stock

1. Add 5 teacups of water to the moong dal, onion and potato and cook in a pressure cooker.
2. When cooked, blend in a blender and pass through a sieve.

How to proceed

1. Heat the butter and sauté the onion and celery for 1 minute.
2. Add the stock and bring to the boil. Simmer for 3 minutes and stir in the dill, salt and pepper.
3. Mix the cornflour with 1 teacup of water and add to the soup.
4. Simmer for another 3 minutes.

✣   **Serve hot.**

✤ CHEESE HOT POT ✤

For the cheese lovers.

| Preparation time : 15 minutes. | Cooking time : 10 minutes. | Serves 6. |

6   teacups brown stock, page 26
1   chopped onion
3   cloves crushed garlic
2   fresh bread slices
1   teacup mixed boiled vegetables
    (french beans, carrots, potatoes,
    cauliflower)

2   tablespoons cooked haricot
    beans (optional)
4   tablespoons grated cheese
2   tablespoons butter
    salt and pepper to taste

1. Heat the butter and sauté the onion and garlic for 1 minute.
2. Add the stock and simmer for 3 minutes.
3. Remove and discard the crust from the bread slices. Crumble the bread and add to the soup.
4. Add the vegetables, beans, cheese, salt and pepper and boil for a few minutes.

✤ Serve hot.

✤ MOONG SOUP WITH PANEER ✤

Light and nutritious.

| Preparation time : 5 minutes. | Cooking time : 25 minutes. | Serves 6. |

¾   teacup moong
2   tablespoons finely chopped paneer

1   teaspoon lemon juice
2   pinches sugar

1	teaspoon cumin seeds	$\frac{1}{4}$	teaspoon pepper powder
1	tablespoon mustard seeds	2	tablespoons ghee
$\frac{1}{4}$	teaspoon asafoetida		salt to taste

1. Soak the moong for a few hours. Add 6 cups of water and cook in a pressure cooker.
2. Blend the cooked moong in a blender. Strain.
3. Heat the ghee and fry the cumin seeds and mustard seeds. When they crackle, add the asafoetida and moong liquid.
4. Add the lemon juice, sugar, salt and pepper and boil for 2 minutes.
5. Add the paneer and cook for 2 minutes.

✤ **Serve hot.**

✤ GOLDEN GLOW SOUP ✤

A soup with a subtle flavour and aroma of vegetables.

Preparation time : 10 minutes.	Cooking time : 45 minutes.	Serves 6.

1 teacup finely chopped mixed boiled vegetables (french beans, potatoes, cauliflower) or 1 teacup mushrooms, sliced (preferably from can)
1 small onion, chopped
1 tablespoon plain flour
3 teacups brown stock, page 26

1 teacup milk
1 tablespoon lemon juice
2 tablespoons butter
   salt and pepper to taste

For the garnish

1 tablespoon chopped parsley

1. Melt the butter in a pan and sauté the onion for a few minutes. Add the vegetables and sauté again for 3 minutes.

Clockwise from top : Bean Sprouts and Radish Salad, page 46; Japanese Salad, Page 29; Maltaise Dressing, Page 65.

2. Add the flour and stock and bring to the boil while stirring continuously. Warm the milk, add to the soup and simmer for 10 minutes. Add the lemon juice, salt and pepper.

❖ **Serve hot, garnished with the chopped parsley.**

❖ HARA NARIEL KA SHORBA ❖

PICTURE ON PAGE 55

Coriander and coconut make a tasty combination.

Preparation time : 20 minutes.	Cooking time : 10 minutes.	Serves 6.

2   coconuts
6   teaspoons cornflour
1   teaspoon cumin seeds
2   tablespoons ghee
2   curry leaves

To be ground into a paste

2   tablespoons chopped coriander
2   small green chillies
1   teaspoon lemon juice

1. Grate the coconut. Add 6 cups of warm water and blend in a blender. Strain to obtain coconut milk.
2. Heat the ghee and fry the cumin seeds for 1 minute. Add the paste and curry leaves and fry again for 1 minute.
3. Mix the cornflour and coconut milk, add to the paste and boil for a few minutes.

❖ **Serve hot.**

◀ *Top: Corn Chowder, page 8; Bottom: Avocado Salad, page 41.*

✤ BEAN SOUP ✤

This piquant soup is ideal for the winter.

Preparation time : 10 minutes.   **Cooking time : 15 minutes.**   **Serves 6.**

1	teacup red kidney beans (rajma)
2	onions, chopped
4	tomatoes, chopped
3	cloves garlic
½	teaspoon chilli powder
1	teaspoon lemon juice
1	tablespoon oil
	salt to taste

For serving

finely chopped tomatoes
sliced green onions
chopped coriander
Tabasco sauce

1. Soak the beans overnight. Drain thoroughly.
2. Heat the oil, add the onions and fry for 1 minute. Add the tomatoes, garlic, chilli powder and salt and fry again for 1 minute.
3. Add the beans and 6 cups of water and cook in a pressure cooker. Blend in a blender.
4. Do not strain. Add the lemon juice.

❖ **Serve hot with tomatoes, onions, coriander and Tabasco sauce.**

✤ HEALTHY TOMATO SOUP ✤

The ever popular tomato soup made in a healthier way.

Preparation time : 5 minutes.   **Cooking time : 25 minutes.**   **Serves 6.**

400 grams chopped tomatoes
½   teacup yellow moong dal
2   teaspoons butter
1   finely chopped onion

1   tablespoon cornflour or
     plain flour
1   to 2 teaspoons sugar
½   teacup warm milk
     salt and pepper to taste

For serving
fresh cream
bread croutons, page 22

1. Boil the tomatoes with the moong dal in 3 to 4 cups of water till cooked.
2. Blend in a blender and strain.
3. Melt the butter, add the onion and fry for 3 to 4 minutes.
4. Add the strained mixture.
5. Mix the cornflour with a little water and pour into the soup. Boil for 2 minutes, stirring ocassionally.
6. Add the sugar, milk, salt and pepper.

✤ **Serve hot with cream and bread croutons.**

SOUP ACCOMPANIMENTS

✣ CROUTONS ✣

Preparation time : 5 minutes.　　　　Cooking time : 5 minutes.

2　slices stale bread
　oil, butter or ghee for frying

1. Remove the crust from the bread slices and cut into small cubes.
2. Heat the oil and fry the bread cubes until golden.
3. Remove, drain well and dry on absorbent paper.

✣ CHEESE CROUTONS ✣

Preparation time : 5 minutes.　　　　Cooking time : 5 minutes.

4　slices bread or a small French roll
100 grams grated cheese (table cheese)

1. Grill the bread slices on one side only.
2. Turn the slices over, sprinkle the cheese on top and grill until golden brown.

Note: Float these croutons on top of the soup just before serving.

VARIATION: Tomato, Capsicum and Cheese Croutons
2　tablespoons finely chopped tomatoes
1　tablespoon finely chopped capsicum
1　tablespoon finely chopped green chillies
100 grams grated cheese (table cheese)

Mix the tomato, capsicum, green chilli and cheese and sprinkle on the ungrilled side of the slices at step 2.

QUICK WHOLE-MEAL
BROWN BREAD ROLLS

Preparation time : 50 minutes.   Cooking time : 15 minutes.   Makes 20 rolls.

250 grams whole wheat flour
10   grams fresh yeast
¾   teaspoon sugar

1   teaspoon butter
¾   teaspoon salt

1. Sieve the flour. Make a well in the centre.
2. Add the yeast, sugar and a little warm water.
3. Wait for at least 4 to 5 minutes or until bubbles come on top.
4. Add the butter and salt, mix well and make a soft dough by adding some more warm water.
5. Knead the dough for 2 minutes.
6. Keep under a wet cloth for 20 minutes. Knead again for 1 minute.
7. Shape into small loaves and put on a well-greased baking tray.
8. Keep the tray in a closed cupboard for 25 minutes or until double in size.
9. Bake in a hot oven at 200°C for 5 minutes. Then reduce the temperature to 150°C and bake a further 10 minutes.
10. Remove from the tin and brush on top with butter.

❖ **Serve hot in folded napkins with butter.**

DAINTY ONION AND JEERA DINNER ROLLS

Preparation time : 50 minutes.   Cooking time : 15 minutes.   Makes 20 rolls.

For the dough

250 grams plain flour
10 grams fresh yeast or 1 teaspoon dry yeast
1   level teaspoon sugar
10 grams soft butter or margarine
1   level teaspoon salt

For the onion mixture

2 teaspoons finely chopped onion
2 teaspoons cumin seeds (jeera)
1 teaspoon ghee

For the onion mixture

Heat the ghee and fry the onion and cumin seeds until golden brown. Keep aside.

For the dough

1. Sieve the flour. Make a well in the centre.
2. Add the yeast, sugar and $\frac{1}{2}$ cup of warm water.
3. Wait for a few minutes until bubbles come on top.
4. Add the butter and salt, mix well and make a soft dough by adding some more warm water.
5. Knead the dough for at least 5 to 6 minutes.

How to proceed

1. Add the onion mixture to the dough and mix well. Keep under a wet cloth for 20 minutes or till the dough doubles in size. Knead again for 1 minute.
2. Shape into very small marble size balls.
3. Put on a well-greased baking tray leaving enough margin for expansion. Keep the tray in a closed cupboard for 20 minutes or until double in size.
4. Bake in a hot oven at 200°C for 5 minutes. Then reduce the temperature to 150°C and bake for a further 10 minutes.
5. Remove from the tin and brush on top with butter.

✤ **Serve hot in folded napkins with butter.**

Note: How to use dry yeast. Put the dry yeast with the sugar in 1 cup of warm water, stir and add a pinch of flour. Cover and leave for 10 minutes. When bubbles come on top, the yeast is ready for use. Then, follow the same method as for fresh yeast.

✤ HERBAL BUTTER ✤

Preparation time : 5 minutes.	No cooking.

2 teaspoons soft butter
1 tablespoon finely chopped parsley or dill

1 tablespoon finely chopped garlic
a few drops lemon juice

Mix the butter, parsley, garlic and lemon juice.

✤ **Serve with dinner rolls and bread.**

✤ WHITE STOCK ✤

Preparation time : 15 minutes.   **Cooking time : 15 minutes.**   **Makes 6 cups.**

1   teacup white pumpkin (lauki) pieces.
2   potatoes
2   onions
    a small piece of cabbage

1. Cut all the vegetables into big pieces.
2. Add 6 cups of water and cook in a pressure cooker.
3. When cooked, blend in a blender and pass through a sieve.

✤ BROWN STOCK ✤

Preparation time : 15 minutes.   **Cooking time : 15 minutes.**   **Makes 6 cups.**

2   carrots   2   large tomatoes
10 french beans   a small piece of cabbage or
1   onion   white pumpkin (lauki)
1   potato

1. Cut all the vegetables into big pieces.
2. Add 6 cups of water and cook in a pressure cooker.
3. When cooked, blend in a blender and pass through a sieve.

Top: Peas and Potato Salad, page 51; Bottom: Spinach and Baby Corn Soup, ▶
page 13.

SALADS

❖ JAPANESE SALAD ❖

PICTURE ON PAGE 17

There couldn't possibly be a better choice than a cream dressing to accompany this delicious salad.

Preparation time : 15 minutes.	No cooking.	Serves 6.

3   teacups lettuce leaves
1   teacup orange segments or
    papaya balls
½   teacup sweet lime segments
½   teacup diced cucumber

For the garnish

6   red cherries (optional)

For the dressing

maltaise dressing, page 65 or
herb cheese dressing, page 70

1. While peeling, handle sweet lime and oranges carefully so that the segments are not mashed.
2. Break the lettuce leaves into bitesize pieces. Do not cut with a knife. Keep in ice-cold water for over 10 minutes. Then shake off all the extra water.
3. Mix the broken lettuce leaves, orange and sweet lime segments and diced cucumber and put in the refrigerator.
4. Just before serving, add the dressing and toss.

❖ **Serve cold on a bed of lettuce leaves, garnished with red cherries.**

Top: Tabbouli, page 32; Bottom: Brown Onion Soup with Pepper Garlic Cheese Balls, page 12.

✤ PINA COLADA SALAD ✤

An excellent combination of chilled rice, fruits and mildly spiced vegetables.

| Preparation time : 20 minutes. | No cooking. | Serves 6. |

½ teacup diced pineapple
½ teacup chopped fresh coconut meat
½ teacup diced capsicum
2 teacups cooked Basmati rice

To be blended into a dressing

¾ teacup coconut milk
3 tablespoons grated coconut
¼ teacup thick fresh cream
a few drops coconut essence
salt and pepper to taste

1. Mix all the salad ingredients in a bowl.
2. Put in the refrigerator.
3. Just before serving, add the dressing and mix well.

✤ **Serve cold on a bed of lettuce leaves.**

✢ ORANGE, GRAPEFRUIT AND MINT SALAD ✢

A minty flavoured salad served with an excellent orange dressing.

| Preparation time : 20 minutes. | No cooking. | Serves 6. |

3 tablespoons orange juice
1½ teacups grapefruit segments
2 teacups orange segments
1 tablespoon sugar
2 mint sprigs, finely chopped

For the garnish

2 mint sprigs

1. Gently heat the orange juice and the sugar in a pan till the sugar dissolves. Cool.
2. Add the chopped mint to the orange syrup.
3. Arrange the orange and grapefruit segments alternately in a dish.
4. Carefully pour the syrup over the fruit. Put in the refrigerator.

✢ **Serve cold, garnished with sprigs of mint.**

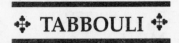 ❖ TABBOULI ❖

PICTURE ON PAGE 28

The Lebanese salad with mint and parsley.

Preparation time : 15 minutes.	Soaking time : 2 hours.	Serves 6.

½ teacup burghul (broken wheat i.e. dalia)

½ teacup finely chopped spring onions

½ teacup chopped mint leaves

½ teacup chopped parsley

1 teacup deseeded and diced tomatoes

To be blended into a dressing

6 tablespoons lemon juice

4 tablespoons olive oil or salad oil
  salt and pepper to taste

1. Soak the burghul in cold water for 2 hours. Drain well and pat dry.
2. Mix the onions, mint, parsley and tomatoes with the burghul.
3. Add the dressing and toss.
4. Put in the refrigerator.

❖ **Serve cold with plain or brown bread.**

✤ SALAD NICOISE ✤

PICTURE ON PAGE 38

The popular French salad modified to suit the vegetarian palate.

Preparation time : 20 minutes.	No cooking.	Serves 6.

2½ teacups broken lettuce leaves
2   tomatoes, cut into quarters
1   teacup boiled green peas
2   tablespoons chopped celery
1   teacup french beans, cooked and cut into cubes
½   teacup sliced capsicum
½   teacup sliced red radish

To be blended into a dressing

1   tablespoon lemon juice
2   tablespoons vinegar
6   tablespoons olive oil or salad oil
1   clove garlic, crushed
½   teaspoon sugar
    salt and pepper to taste

For the garnish

6   stuffed black olives
½   teacup cottage cheese cubes
    lettuce leaves

1. Mix all the salad ingredients in a bowl.
2. Add the dressing and toss.
3   Arrange in a bowl and garnish with the olives and cottage cheese cubes.
4. Put in the refrigerator.

✤ **Serve cold, surrounded by lettuce leaves.**

✤ GADO GADO ✤

PICTURE ON PAGE 38

The famous Indonesian salad served with a rich peanut sauce.

Preparation time : 15 minutes.	No cooking.	Serves 6.

2   potatoes, boiled and diced
1   teacup french beans, boiled
    and diced
¼   teacup carrots, boiled and diced
1   cucumber, sliced
1   teacup bean sprouts,
    washed and drained
¼   teacup boiled green peas

For the dressing

spicy peanut sauce, page 69

For the garnish

fried mini papads

1. Mix all the salad ingredients in a bowl.
2. Add the peanut sauce and toss.
3. Put in the refrigerator.

✤ **Serve cold, surrounded with fried mini papads.**

34

✤ TROPICAL INDIAN SALAD ✤

A colourful mixture of fruit and vegetables served with a rich mango dressing.

Preparation time : 25 minutes.	No cooking.	Serves 6 to 8.

1 small can (450 grams)
   pineapple titbits or scooped out
   portion of one pineapple
2 apples, cut into cubes
2 bananas, cut into cubes

1 cucumber, cut into cubes
2 big tomatoes, cut into
   quarters (remove the
   pulp and seeds)
2 capsicums
2 oranges, segmented

For the dressing

mango dressing, page 70, or thousand island dressing, page 64

For the decoration

pineapple slices
cherries
lettuce leaves

For serving the dressing

1 scooped out pineapple shell

1. Mix all the salad ingredients and put in the refrigerator.
2. Just before serving, drain and place in the centre on a large platter.
3. Surround with pineapple slices and decorate with cherries and lettuce leaves.

✤ **Pour the dressing into the pineapple shell and serve cold with the salad.**

✛ CARROT AND DATE SALAD ✛

PICTURE ON PAGE 37

A healthy combination of carrots and dates.

Preparation time : 15 minutes.	No cooking.	Serves 6 to 8.

2   teacups grated carrots
1   head lettuce
½   teacup chopped dates
2   tablespoons chopped toasted
    almonds (optional)

For the dressing

honey and lemon dressing,
page 66

1. Put the carrots in ice-cold water for 10 minutes. Drain thoroughly.
2. Put the lettuce in ice-cold water for 10 minutes. Drain thoroughly.
3. Break off the individual lettuce leaves into bitesize pieces and prepare a bed of the leaves in a serving bowl.
4. Spread the grated carrots in the middle.
5. Sprinkle the chopped dates and toasted almonds over the carrots.
6. Put in the refrigerator.

✛ **Serve cold with the dressing in a separate bowl.**

Clockwise from top: Carrot and Date Salad, above ; Creamy Almond Soup, page 11; Melon and Papaya Balls in Honey and Ginger Dressing, page 49.

✤ FLORIDA SALAD ✤

A favourite combination of fruit and cheese.

Preparation time : 25 minutes.	No cooking.	Serves 6.

2 teacups pears or any
　other fruit, diced
1 teacup paneer cubes
½ teacup finely diced capsicum
1 head lettuce
2 cucumbers, thinly sliced

To be blended into a dressing

1 tablespoon lemon juice
1 tablespoon white vinegar
6 tablespoons olive oil or salad oil
1 tablespoon finely chopped
　parsley
　freshly ground pepper and
　salt to taste

For the garnish

½ teacup bread croutons, page 22
6 red cherries

1. If using fresh pears, sprinkle a little lemon juice on top to avoid discolouring.
2. Mix the capsicum with the pears and paneer cubes.
3. Put the lettuce in ice-cold water for 10 minutes. Drain thoroughly.
4. Break the lettuce into bitesize pieces and arrange on a round platter.
5. Pile the pear and paneer mixture in the centre and make a ring of the cucumber slices on the outside.
6. Sprinkle the croutons around the salad and top with the cherries.
7. Put in the refrigerator.

✤ Just before serving, sprinkle the dressing on top. Serve cold.

Note: You can also serve this salad with maltaise dressing, page 65.

◀ *Top: Salad Niçoise, page 33; Bottom; Gado Gado, page 34.*

✤ EVE'S SALAD ✤

An age-old favourite combination of apples and celery along with other easily available fruits.

Preparation time : 20 minutes.	No cooking.	Serves 6.

½ teacup black grapes
2 teacups apple cubes
1½ teacups pineapple cubes
½ teacup banana cubes
1 teaspoon lemon juice

For the dressing

sour cream dressing, page 69, or
herb cheese dressing, page 70

For the garnish

2 tablespoons chopped walnuts
1 tablespoon chopped celery
1 sweet lime or orange, sliced (with the skin on)

1. Sprinkle the lemon juice over the apple cubes to avoid discolouring.
2. Mix all the salad ingredients in a bowl.
3. Add the dressing and toss.
4. Garnish with the walnuts and celery.
5. Surround the salad with sweet lime or orange slices.
6. Put in the refrigerator.

✤ **Serve cold.**

✤ AVOCADO SALAD ✤

PICTURE ON PAGE 18

An excellent combination of avocado and baby corn served with a honey and lemon dressing.

Preparation time : 20 minutes.	No cooking.	Serves 6.

1 large avocado, sliced
2 capsicums
2 tomatoes, deseeded
8 to 10 pieces baby corn
2 cucumbers

To be blended into a dressing

4 tablespoons honey
1½ tablespoons lemon juice
2 teaspoons finely chopped mint leaves
½ teaspoon crushed pepper
salt to taste

1. Gently peel and slice the avocado. Keep aside a few slices for decoration.
2. Cut the capsicum, tomatoes, baby corn and cucumber into long strips.
3. Blanch the baby corn in boiling water for a few minutes. Drain.
4. Mix the vegetables and the avocado slices in a large plate.
5. Add the dressing and put in the refrigerator.

✤ **Serve cold, decorated with the remaining avocado slices.**

✤ JUMBO HOTCHPOTCH SALAD ✤

PICTURE ON BACK COVER

Let your imagination run wild! Create your own combinations of salads and dressings!

Preparation time : 25 minutes.	No cooking.	Serves 6.

Mix any combination of the following vegetables and fruits (it is important that they should be fresh) with any of the following dressings:

Vegetables and Fruits

baby corn
bean sprouts
beetroot
carrots
cucumbers
mushrooms
oranges
red radish
spring onions
tomatoes
watercress
lettuce

Dressings

vinaigrette dressing, page 68
green goddess, page 65
cheese dressing, page 68
spicy peanut sauce, page 69
minty honey dressing, page 67
low calorie dressing, page 71

Cut the fresh vegetables and fruits into strips, cubes, slices etc. as you like. Put in the refrigerator.

✤ **Serve cold with any desired dressing.**

✤ ITALIANO SALAD ✤

PICTURE ON PAGE 56

This oregano-flavoured macaroni salad is sure to please pasta lovers.

Preparation time : 20 minutes.	Cooking time : 15 minutes.	Serves 6.

1 teacup macaroni
1 tomato, deseeded and diced
1 capsicum, diced
3 spring onions with greens, chopped
2 tablespoons oil

For the dressing

vinaigrette dressing, page 68 , with ½ teaspoon oregano or curry sauce, page 67

For the garnish

5 to 6 stuffed olives, cut into halves

1. Boil the macaroni in sufficient water along with ½ teaspoon of salt and 1 tablespoon of oil. Drain thoroughly, wash and cool.
2. Add the remaining salad ingredients and mix.
3. Put in the refrigerator.
4. Just before serving, add the dressing and toss.

✤ **Serve cold, garnished with olives.**

✤ AMERICAN SWEET CORN SALAD ✤

PICTURE ON PAGE 56

Your all-time favourite. Sweet corn blends well with the flabour of spring onions.

| Preparation time : 10 minutes. | No cooking. | Serves 6. |

2 teacups sweet corn
½ teacup diced spring onions
   (with green stems)
½ teacup diced capsicum
½ teacup diced tomato

For the dressing

vinaigrette dressing, page 68

1. Keep aside half the tomatoes and spring onion greens and mix the remaining salad ingredients.
2. Toss in the dressing.
3. Garnish with the remaining tomatoes and spring onions.
4. Put in the refrigerator.

✤ **Serve cold.**

✤ BEAN SPROUTS SALAD ✤

Healthy, colourful, crunchy and easy-to-make.

| Preparation time : 15 minutes. | No cooking. | Serves 6. |

2 teacups bean sprouts
(washed and drained)
2 teacups cucumbers sliced in
half lengthwise,
seeded and cut like matchsticks
½ teacup diced spring onions
(with green stems)

For the dressing

2 tablespoons vinegar
1 tablespoon castor sugar
2 tablespoons oil
½ teaspoon mustard powder
salt and pepper to taste

For the garnish

3 tablespoons roasted peanuts

For the dressing

Shake the ingredients thoroughly in a closed bottle.

How to proceed

1. Combine the bean sprouts, cucumber and onions.
2. Put in the refrigerator.
3. Just before serving, add the dressing and toss.

✤ **Serve cold, garnished with roasted peanuts.**

❖ BEAN SPROUTS AND RADISH SALAD ❖

PICTURE ON PAGE 17

A nourishing, healthy salad with the sharpness of red radishes.

Preparation time : 10 minutes.	No cooking.	Serves 6.

2　teacups bean sprouts
　　(washed and drained)
1　capsicum, cut into strips
4　red radishes, sliced
¾　teacup diagonally sliced
　　spring onions

For the garnish

½　teacup black olives or stuffed
　　olives
1　tomato, cored and sliced into
　　rings

For the dressing

2　teaspoons vinegar
2　tablespoons olive oil or salad oil
2　teaspoons lemon juice
1　clove garlic, crushed
½　teaspoon soya sauce
½　teaspoon sugar
　　salt and pepper to taste

For the dressing

Shake the ingredients thoroughly in a closed bottle.

How to proceed

1. Mix the bean sprouts, capsicum, radishes and spring onions in a bowl.
2. Put in the refrigerator.
3. Just before serving, pour the dressing over the salad and toss.

❖ **Serve cold, garnished with olives on top and tomato rings on the sides.**

❖ THREE BEAN SALAD ❖

PICTURE ON PAGE 56

An excellent combination of mixed beans tossed in chaat masala dressing.

Preparation time : 10 minutes.	No cooking.	Serves 6.

3 teacups mixed boiled beans
(choose from rajma, chowli,
chick peas, lima beans or
hare chana)
½ teacup spring onions,
cut into rings
¾ teacup diced tomatoes
1 teaspoon chopped green chillies
2 tablespoons chopped coriander

To be mixed into a dressing
¼ teacup lemon juice
2 teaspoons chaat masala
powder
¼ teaspoon black salt
salt and pepper to taste

1. Keeping aside half the coriander leaves for garnishing, mix all the salad ingredients.
2. Toss in the dressing and put in the refrigerator.

❖ **Serve cold, garnished with the balance coriander.**

✥ CURRIED PASTA AND BEAN SALAD ✥

Curry powder imparts a special flavour to pasta and beans.

Preparation time : 10 minutes.   **Cooking time : 25 minutes.**   **Serves 6.**

1   teacup kidney beans or haricot beans
¾   teacup shell pasta
2   tablespoons chopped dill leaves
1   clove garlic, crushed
2   teaspoons oil
      salt and pepper to taste

To be blended into a dressing

½   teacup creamy mayonnaise, page 72
1   teaspoon curry powder
½   teaspoon salt
      white pepper to taste

For the garnish

fried bread croutons, page 22
2   tablespoons chopped parsley

1. Soak the beans overnight. Next day, cook with salt in a pressure cooker, making sure not to overcook the beans. Drain thoroughly.
2 Put plenty of water to boil, add the oil and salt. Add the pasta and cook till just done. Drain well and plunge in cold water.
3. Mix all the salad ingredients and put in the refrigerator.
4. Just before serving, add the dressing and toss.

✥ **Serve cold, garnished with croutons and chopped parsley.**

MELON AND PAPAYA BALLS IN HONEY AND GINGER DRESSING

PICTURE ON PAGE 37

A sweet chilled salad for hot summer days.

Preparation time : 15 minutes.	No cooking.	Serves 6.

2 teacups papaya balls
   (preferably the red variety)
2 teacups honeydew melon balls
2 teacups watermelon balls

To be blended into a honey-ginger dressing

3   tablespoons honey
1   teaspoon lemon juice
2   teaspoons ginger juice
¼   teaspoon crushed pepper
    salt to taste

For the garnish

a mint sprig

1. While scooping out the fruits, put the balls in ice-cold water. After 10 minutes, drain thoroughly.
2. Arrange all the balls carefully in a bowl in such a way that they do not get mashed.
3. Pour the dressing evenly over the bowl.
4 Put in the refrigerator.

❖ **Serve cold, garnished with a sprig of mint in the centre.**

BROCCOLI AND PEACHES WITH CHEESE DRESSING

Luscious and delicious.

Preparation time : 10 minutes.   **Cooking time : 5 minutes.**   **Serves 4 to 6.**

2 teacups broccoli florets
4 peaches or 1 large can
   (450 grams) peaches

For the dressing

cheese dressing, page 68, or
thousand island dressing, page 64

For the garnish

toasted almond slivers

1. Blanch the broccoli in boiling water for 3 minutes. Drain and place in ice-cold water for 10 to 15 minutes.
2. Slice the peaches. If using from can, drain thoroughly.
3. Arrange the broccoli and peaches in a bowl and pour the dressing on top. Put in the refrigerator.

❖ **Serve cold, garnished with almond slivers.**

✤ PEAS AND POTATO SALAD ✤

PICTURE ON PAGE 27

A mild, pleasantly flavoured dill sauce transforms this simple salad of peas and potatoes.

Preparation time : 15 minutes.   **Cooking time : 10 minutes.**   **Serves 6.**

2   teacups baby potatoes
1   teacup fresh green peas

For the dressing

dill sauce, page 66

For the garnish

2   tablespoons chopped fresh dill leaves

1. Peel and boil the potatoes and store in salted cold water.
2. Cook the peas lightly in boiling water.
3. Put the potatoes and peas in a serving bowl. Add the sauce and toss.
4. Put in the refrigerator.

✤ **Serve cold, garnished with dill leaves.**

✤ SPANISH SALAD ✤

A basil flavoured dressing complements the mushrooms very well in this salad.

| Preparation time : 20 minutes. | No cooking. | Serves 6. |

½ teacup sliced onions
¼ teacup sliced capsicum
2 teacups sliced mushrooms
(canned or fresh)
¼ teacup gherkins, cut like
matchsticks (optional)
2 fresh red tomatoes
¾ teacup french beans
2 tablespoons lemon juice
(if using fresh mushrooms)

To be blended into a dressing

1 tablespoon lemon juice
2 tablespoons olive oil or
salad oil
½ teaspoon dried basil or tulsi
leaves

For the garnish

stuffed olives, cut into half

1. If using fresh mushrooms, put them for 10 minutes in water mixed with the lemon juice. Drain.
2. Cut each tomato into four parts.
3. Cut the french beans into cubes or diamonds. Blanch in boiling salted water for 5 minutes. Drain and refresh in ice-cold water. Drain thoroughly.
4. Mix all the salad ingredients and put in the refrigerator.
5. Just before serving, add the dressing to the salad and toss.

✤ **Serve cold, garnished with stuffed olives.**

❖ PANEER AUR HARE CHANE KA SALAD ❖

PICTURE ON PAGE 55

Paneer and chane tossed in an Indian lemon-based dressing.

Preparation time : 15 minutes.	No cooking.	Serves 6 to 8.

$1\frac{1}{2}$ teacups dried hare chane,
soaked and boiled

1 teacup diced tomatoes

$\frac{3}{4}$ teacup diced paneer

$\frac{1}{2}$ teacup chopped spring
onions (optional)

For the garnish

3 tablespoons chopped
coriander

To be blended into a dressing

4 tablespoons lemon juice

$\frac{1}{2}$ teaspoon chaat masala

$\frac{1}{2}$ teaspoon cumin seeds,
roasted and coarsely ground

$\frac{1}{4}$ teaspoon black salt
salt and pepper to taste

1. Place all the salad ingredients in a mixing bowl, taking care to handle the paneer carefully so that it is not mashed.
2. Add the dressing and toss gently in a bowl.

❖ **Serve garnished with the coriander.**

Note: When fresh hare chane is in season, use the chane after blanching for a few minutes in salted water.

✛ SWEET CORN AND KIDNEY BEAN SALAD ✛

A colourful and tasty salad that is simple to make.

Preparation time : a few minutes.	No cooking.	Serves 6.

2 teacups cooked kidney
beans (rajma)
2 teacups cooked fresh corn
(preferably sweet corn)
1 small onion, chopped
salt and pepper to taste

For the dressing

vinaigrette dressing, page 68 ,
or low calorie dressing, page 71

1. Mix all the salad ingredients in a bowl.
2. Put in the refrigerator.
3. Just before serving, add the dressing and toss.

✛ **Serve cold**.

Top: Paneer aur Hare Chane ka Salad, page 53; Bottom: Hara Nariel ka Shorba , page 19.

➤

✤ VEGETABLE GARDEN SALAD WITH NUTS ✤

Sesame seeds and almonds enhance the taste of this salad.

| Preparation time : 15 minutes. | Cooking time : 15 minutes. | Serves 6. |

250 grams cauliflower florets
250 grams young carrots
250 grams french beans

For the spicy almond powder

3 tablespoons sesame seeds
2 tablespoons blanched and
   sliced almonds
   salt and pepper to taste

For the dressing

vinaigrette dressing, page 68, or
low calorie dressing, page 71

For the spicy almond powder

1. Lightly roast the sesame seeds and almonds on a medium flame while stirring constantly.
2. Grind the roasted sesame seeds and almonds coarsely in a coffee grinder.
3. Add salt and pepper and mix.

How to proceed

1. Cut the carrots into thin rounds.
2. Cut the french beans diagonally into pieces of about 25 mm. width.
3. Put plenty of water to boil with salt. Add the vegetables and cook for a few minutes. Drain and put immediately in cold water for 10 to 15 minutes. Drain thoroughly.
4. Put the vegetables in a mixing bowl and put in the refrigerator.
5. Just before serving, add the dressing and toss.

✤ **Sprinkle the spicy almond powder on top and serve cold.**

Clockwise from top: American Sweet Corn Salad, page 44; Assorted Pickles, page 63; Three Bean Salad, page 47; Italiano Salad, page 43; Beetroot and Dill Salad, page 60.

BROCCOLI, BEAN SPROUTS AND GREEN PEAS SALAD

An East and West salad. The sesame seeds add a unique taste to the salad.

Preparation time : 45 minutes.   **Cooking time : 15 minutes.**   **Serves 6.**

2 teacups broccoli florets
2 teacups bean sprouts
1 teacup green peas
3 spring onions

To be mixed into a dressing

2 tablespoons lemon juice
2 tablespoons salad oil
1 tablespoon soya sauce
2 teaspoons powdered sugar
¼ teaspoon pepper

For the garnish

1 tablespoon sesame seeds

1. Put plenty of water to boil with salt. Add the broccoli and cook for 1 minute. Drain and put immediately in cold water for 10 to 15 minutes. Drain thoroughly.
2. Cook the green peas in boiling salted water for 3 to 4 minutes. Drain and put immediately in cold water for at least half an hour. Drain thoroughly. See that the peas remain crisp.
3. Put the bean sprouts in cold water for 10 minutes. Drain thoroughly.
4. Put the broccoli, green peas, bean sprouts and spring onions in a bowl and put in the refrigerator.
5. Just before serving, add the dressing and toss.

❖ **Serve cold, topped with the sesame seeds.**

✥ CELERY, CUCUMBER AND GRAPE SALAD ✥

A colourful and crunchy salad.

| Preparation time : a few minutes. | No cooking. | Serves 4. |

1 teacup chopped celery (without leaves)
1 teacup diced cucumber
2 teacups seedless grapes, halved

For the dressing

¾ teacup fresh curds
1 teaspoon honey
1 teaspoon made mustard
   salt and pepper to taste

For the decoration

crisp lettuce leaves

1. Put all the salad ingredients in a bowl. Put in the refrigerator.
2. Mix all the ingredients for the dressing.
3. Just before serving, pour over the salad and mix well.

✥ **Serve cold on a bed of crisp lettuce leaves.**

✤ BEETROOT AND DILL SALAD ✤

PICTURE ON PAGE 56

An energy-giving salad, rich in vitamins.

Preparation time : a few minutes.	No cooking.	Serves 4.

4   medium-sized beetroots, boiled
2   tablespoons chopped fresh dill

For the dressing

vinaigrette dressing, page 68

1. Cut the beetroots into small cubes. Add the dressing and put in the refrigerator.
2. Just before serving, add the dill leaves.

✤ **Serve cold.**

✤ ZESTY BANANA SALAD ✤

Crunchy, sweet and sour.

Preparation time : 10 minutes.	No cooking.	Serves 4.

3   large ripe bananas, sliced
2   tablespoons lemon juice
1   cucumber, sliced
1   tablespoon chopped dill
¼   small green chilli, chopped

¼   teacup coarsely chopped peanuts
1   teacup yoghurt or fresh curds
2   teaspoons chopped fresh mint leaves
    salt and pepper to taste

1. Put the bananas in a large bowl, sprinkle the lemon juice on top and wait for 5 minutes.
2. Add the cucumber, dill, green chilli and peanuts.
3. Mix the yoghurt, mint, salt and pepper in a bowl. Add the banana mixture and mix well.
4. Place in the refrigerator.

❖ Serve cold.

❖ LA FIESTA ❖

An interesting colourful salad.

Preparation time : 10 minutes.　　　**No cooking.**　　　**Serves 4 to 6.**

1 teacup tomatoes, cut into large pieces
1 teacup capsicum, cut into chunks
2 teacups fresh pineapple pieces
2 teacups apple pieces (unpeeled)
2 spring onions, chopped
1 teacup celery sticks, chopped

For the dressing

vinaigrette dressing, page 68 , or
thousand island dressing, page 64

To serve

lettuce leaves

1. Mix all the salad ingredients and put in the refrigerator.
2. Just before serving, add the dressing and toss.

❖ **Serve cold on a bed of lettuce leaves.**

✦ FRENCH BEANS WITH SESAME SEEDS ✦

The everyday healthy salad.

Preparation time : 10 minutes.	Cooking time : 5 minutes.	Serves 4.

2 teacups french beans, sliced
1 teacup green cucumber,
   cut into big pieces
2 tablespoons celery chunks
2 tablespoons sesame seeds,
   roasted

For the dressing
vinaigrette dressing, page 68

To serve
lettuce leaves

1. Cook the french beans in boiling water for 2 to 3 minutes until crisp. Remove and drain.
2. Add the cucumber and the celery and put in the refrigerator.
3. Just before serving, add the dressing and toss. Sprinkle sesame seeds on top.

✦ **Serve cold in individual lettuce cups.**

✦ ASSORTED PICKLES ✦

PICTURE ON PAGE 56

These easy-to-make pickles last for several months. They can be used in various ways, eaten as a pickle, salad or served as an accompaniment to the meal.

Preparation time : 5 minutes.   **Cooking time : 5 minutes.**

1 teacup whole baby corn
1 teacup carrot sticks
1 teacup beetroot sticks
1 teacup boiled cocktail onions

For the marinade

3   teacups water
1   teacup vinegar
¾ teacup sugar
½ teaspoon salt
10 to 12 peppercorns
4   bay leaves

For the marinade

Mix all the ingredients including the water and put to boil. Once it boils, divide into 4 equal parts.

For the assorted pickles

1. Add one vegetable to each portion of the marinade and cook till the vegetables are slightly tender.
2. Cool and store in airtight jars.

SALAD DRESSINGS

❖ THOUSAND ISLAND DRESSING ❖

The popular American dressing.

Preparation time : 5 minutes.	No cooking.	Makes 1-1/4 cups.

200 grams fresh cream
3 tablespoons thick curds
3 tablespoons tomato ketchup
½ teaspoon chilli sauce
2 teaspoons chopped onion
2 teaspoons chopped capsicum

¼ teaspoon chopped green chillies
1 level teaspoon mustard powder
1 tablespoon powdered sugar
salt to taste

1. Beat the cream until thick.
2. Add the remaining ingredients and mix well.
3. Store in the refrigerator and use within 12 hours.

❖ **Serve cold.**

❖ GREEN GODDESS ❖

This thick dressing goes very well with greens.

Preparation time : 5 minutes.	No cooking.	Makes 1 cup.

¾ teacup hung curds
1½ teaspoons chopped parsley
1 teaspoon dill

½ teaspoon chopped basil or tulsi
¼ teacup fresh cream
salt and pepper to taste

1. Mix all the ingredients.
2. Store in the refrigerator and use within 12 hours.

❖ **Serve cold.**

Note: Curds should be tied in muslin cloth and hung for at least 4 hours to remove water.

❖ MALTAISE DRESSING ❖

PICTURE ON PAGE 17

This creamy orange dressing goes very well with fruit salad.

Preparation time : a few minutes.	No cooking.	Makes 1 cup.

¾ teacup fresh cream
3 tablespoons orange squash
1 teacup castor sugar

¼ teaspoon grated orange rind
salt and pepper to taste

1. Mix all the ingredients.
2. Store in the refrigerator and use within 24 hours.

❖ **Serve cold.**

✧ HONEY AND LEMON DRESSING ✧

The dressing should be served at room temperature.

Preparation time : a few minutes.	No cooking.	Makes 1 cup.

¾ teacup honey
3 tablespoons lemon juice
½ teaspoon freshly crushed peppercorn

When required for use, mix all the ingredients in a blender.

✧ DILL SAUCE ✧

If you want a thinner dressing, increase the quantity of cream.

Preparation time : a few minutes.	No cooking.	Makes 1 cup.

2 tablespoons chopped dill leaves
¾ teacup hung curds
1 teaspoon lemon juice

3 tablespoons fresh cream
salt and pepper to taste

1. Mix all the ingredients.
2. Store in the refrigerator and use within 12 hours.

✧ **Serve cold.**

Note: Curds should be tied in muslin cloth and hung for at least 4 hours to remove water.

❖ CURRY SAUCE ❖

Goes very well with pasta.

Preparation time : a few minutes.	No cooking.	Makes 1 cup.

1 teacup creamy mayonnaise, page 72
1 tablespoon curry powder
   salt and pepper to taste

1. Mix all the ingredients in a blender.
2. Store in the refrigerator and use within 2 days.
3. Whisk well before using.

❖ **Serve cold.**

❖ MINTY HONEY DRESSING ❖

Use this dressing in salads containing fruits.

Preparation time : a few minutes.	No cooking.	Makes 1 cup.

½ teacup honey
3 tablespoons chopped mint
1 tablespoon vinegar
   salt and pepper to taste

1. Mix all the ingredients in a blender.
2. Store in the refrigerator and use within 2 days.

❖ **Serve cold.**

✤ VINAIGRETTE DRESSING ✤

This sour dressing can be kept for a long time without spoilage.

Preparation time : a few minutes.	No cooking.	Makes 1 cup.

$\frac{3}{4}$ teacup salad oil
$\frac{1}{4}$ teacup vinegar
$\frac{1}{4}$ teaspoon mustard powder

$\frac{1}{2}$ teaspoon sugar
salt and pepper to taste

1. Put all the ingredients in a closed bottle and shake well.
2. Store in a cool place.
3. Just before use, shake well.

Note: If you wish, you can add chopped parsley and gherkins to highlight the sour tinge in this dressing.

✤ CHEESE DRESSING ✤

For the cheese lovers.

Preparation time : 5 minutes.	No cooking.	Makes 1 cup.

$\frac{1}{4}$ teacup grated cheese or cheese spread
$\frac{1}{2}$ teacup creamy mayonnaise, page 72, or yoghurt

$\frac{1}{4}$ teacup fresh cream
a pinch black pepper
salt to taste

1. Mix all the ingredients in a blender.
2. Store in the refrigerator and use within 24 hours.

✤ **Serve cold.**

✤ SOUR CREAM DRESSING ✤

Delicately sour.

Preparation time : a few minutes.	No cooking.	Makes 1 cup.

1 teacup cream
2 tablespoons lemon juice or 2 tablespoons thick curds
   salt and pepper to taste

1. Beat the cream lightly.
2. Add the ingredients and mix.
3. Store in the refrigerator and use within 24 hours.

✤ Serve cold.

✤ SPICY PEANUT SAUCE ✤

A sauce with the taste of peanut butter.

Preparation time : 5 minutes.	No cooking.	Makes 1 cup.

1 teacup roasted peanuts   ½ teaspoon chilli powder
1 tablespoon jaggery (gur)   ½ teacup water
1 tablespoon tamarind water   salt to taste

1. Mix all the ingredients in a blender.
2. Store in the refrigerator and use within 4 days.

✤ Serve cold.

✣ MANGO DRESSING ✣

An unusual dressing.

Preparation time : 5 minutes.	No cooking.	Makes 2 cups.

1	teacup mango pulp	2	cardamons, powdered
1	teacup fresh curds		a pinch chilli powder
2	tablespoons fresh cream		salt and pepper to taste

1. Mix all the ingredients in a blender until smooth.
2. Taste the sauce and adjust the seasoning as required.
3. Store in the refrigerator and use within 12 hours.

✣ **Serve cold.**

✣ HERB CHEESE DRESSING ✣

Serve as a dip with raw vegetables.

Preparation time : 5 minutes.	No cooking.	Makes 1 cup.

¾	teacup grated cottage cheese or paneer	1	tablespoon chopped fresh dill
2	tablespoons fresh curds	1	tablespoon chopped chives (optional)
2	tablespoons chopped parsley	½	teaspoon salt

1. Mix all the ingredients in a blender. If you find the mixture too thick, add some fresh curds.
2. Store in the refrigerator and use within 12 hours.

✣ **Serve cold.**

70

✤ LOW CALORIE DRESSING ✤

For the dieters.

Preparation time : 5 minutes.   **Cooking time : 3 minutes.**   **Makes 1 cup.**

2 teaspoons cornflour
1 tablespoon finely chopped onion
¼ teacup vinegar
¼ teacup tomato ketchup
2 tablespoons vegetable oil
1½ teaspoons sugar

½ teaspoon prepared mustard
¼ teaspoon chilli powder
1 clove garlic, crushed
    (optional)
½ teaspoon Worcestershire
    sauce
½ teaspoon salt

1. Mix the cornflour with ¾ cup of water in a saucepan and cook over medium heat until the mixture is clear and thick. Cool.
2. Add the remaining ingredients, put in a jar and shake well.
3. Store in the refrigerator and use within 4 days.

✤ **Serve cold.**

71

❖ CREAMY MAYONNAISE ❖

The ever popular dressing.

Preparation time : a few minutes.   No cooking.   Makes about $1\frac{1}{4}$ teacups.

200	grams fresh cream	3	teaspoons lemon juice
2	tablespoons salad oil or refined oil	$\frac{1}{4}$	teaspoon pepper
1	teaspoon mustard powder	$\frac{1}{2}$	teaspoon salt
3	teaspoons powdered sugar		

1. Beat the cream until thick.
2. Add the remaining ingredients and mix well.
3. Store in the refrigerator and use within 24 hours.

❖ **Serve cold.**